SUPERPOWER SCIENCE

MASTERS OF MATTER

JOY LIN

ILLUSTRATED BY
ALAN BROWN

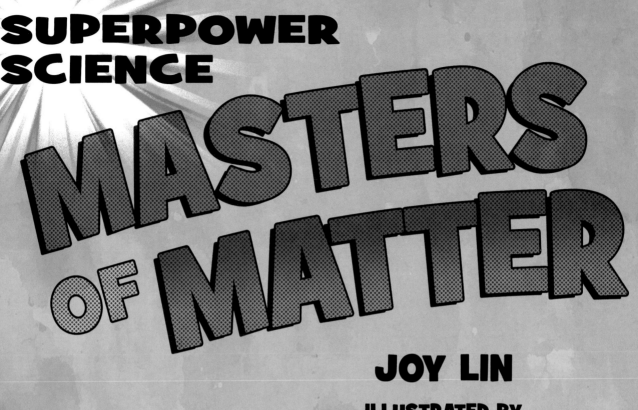

B.E.S.
PUBLISHING

FIRST EDITION FOR THE UNITED STATES, ITS
TERRITORIES AND DEPENDENCIES, THE PHILIPPINE
REPUBLIC, AND CANADA PUBLISHED IN 2019 BY
B.E.S. PUBLISHING CO.

TEXT COPYRIGHT © JOY LIN, 2018
ART AND DESIGN COPYRIGHT © HODDER & STOUGHTON, 2018
FIRST PUBLISHED IN GREAT BRITAIN IN 2018 BY
WAYLAND, AN IMPRINT OF HACHETTE CHILDREN'S
GROUP, PART OF HODDER & STOUGHTON.

ALL INQUIRIES SHOULD BE ADDRESSED TO:
B.E.S. PUBLISHING CO.
250 WIRELESS BOULEVARD
HAUPPAUGE, NY 11788
WWW.BES-PUBLISHING.COM

ISBN: 978-1-4380-1267-4

LIBRARY OF CONGRESS CONTROL NUMBER: 2018951834

DATE OF MANUFACTURE: JANUARY 2019
MANUFACTURED BY: WKT, SHENZHEN, CHINA

PRINTED IN CHINA
9 8 7 6 5 4 3 2 1

What if I had a superpower?

HAVEN'T WE ALL ASKED OURSELVES THIS QUESTION AT SOME POINT? IT WOULD BE AMAZING TO BE ABLE TO GROW OR SHRINK, TELEPORT, OR SHAPE-SHIFT. ARE THESE ABILITIES THE STUFF OF DREAMS OR WILL WE ONE DAY BE ABLE TO BE REAL-LIFE SUPERHEROES?

ONCE UPON A TIME WE WERE ONLY ABLE TO OBSERVE THE STARS FROM EARTH AND DREAM OF EXPLORING SPACE, THEN ONE DAY, WE SENT MEN TO THE MOON! SCIENCE IS DEFINITELY CATCHING UP WITH OUR IMAGINATIONS. LET'S SEE WHAT HAPPENS WHEN YOU APPLY THE LAWS OF SCIENCE TO SUPERPOWERS...

CONTENTS

WHAT IS MATTER?

First, we need to look at matter: matter is defined as anything that takes up space and has mass (the amount of stuff an object contains). So a lamp, an oven, and a bell all count as matter.

HOWEVER, THE LIGHT FROM THE LAMP, THE HEAT FROM THE OVEN, AND THE SOUND FROM THE BELL DO NOT BECAUSE THEY DO NOT HAVE MASS.

THE THREE MAIN STATES OF MATTER ARE *SOLID*, *LIQUID*, AND *GAS*. ALL MATTER IS MADE UP OF DIFFERENT KINDS OF ATOMS, WHICH ARE THE BUILDING BLOCKS OF MATTER. ATOMS BONDED TOGETHER ARE CALLED MOLECULES. FOR EXAMPLE, A WATER MOLECULE (H_2O) CONSISTS OF TWO HYDROGEN ATOMS AND AN OXYGEN ATOM.

IN *SOLIDS*, THE ATOMS ARE STACKED UP RIGHT NEXT TO EACH OTHER AND THEY CAN BARELY MOVE. IMAGINE AN ELEVATOR PACKED TO ITS FULL CAPACITY (THE PEOPLE IN THE ELEVATOR ARE THE ATOMS), THAT'S HOW TIGHT THE ATOMS IN SOLIDS ARE PACKED TOGETHER.

IN *LIQUIDS*, THE ATOMS ARE STILL RELATIVELY CLOSE, BUT THERE IS ENOUGH SPACE FOR THEM TO MOVE AROUND.

IN *GASES*, THE MOLECULES HAVE LOTS OF ROOM TO ROAM AROUND AT HIGH SPEEDS.

Solids, Liquids, and Gases Can Change State

WHEN A *SOLID* TURNS INTO A *LIQUID*, IT'S CALLED *FUSION*, OR MELTING. AN ICE CUBE MELTS INTO WATER WHEN IT ABSORBS HEAT FROM ITS SURROUNDINGS.

WHEN A *SOLID* TURNS INTO A *GAS*, IT'S CALLED *SUBLIMATION*. SOLID CO_2, COMMONLY KNOWN AS DRY ICE, SUBLIMES AT ROOM TEMPERATURE.

WHEN A *LIQUID* TURNS INTO A *GAS*, IT'S CALLED *EVAPORATION*, OR BOILING. WATER BOILS AT 212°F (100°C) AND TURNS INTO WATER VAPOR, ALSO CALLED STEAM.

WHEN A *GAS* TURNS INTO A *LIQUID*, IT'S CALLED *CONDENSATION*. THE COLD WINDOW IN THE BATHROOM CONDENSES THE STEAM FROM YOUR SHOWER BACK INTO WATER.

WHEN A *LIQUID* TURNS INTO A *SOLID*, IT'S CALLED *FREEZING*. FRUIT JUICE CAN BE FROZEN INTO TASTY POPSICLES.

FINALLY, WHEN A *GAS* TURNS INTO A *SOLID*, IT'S CALLED *DEPOSITION*. ON WINTER MORNINGS, WATER VAPOR IN THE AIR CAN TURN STRAIGHT INTO FROST WITHOUT BECOMING A LIQUID FIRST.

The Law of Conservation of Mass

IF I MELT AN ICE CUBE THAT WEIGHS HALF AN OUNCE (10 G), I SHOULD GET HALF AN OUNCE (10 G) OF WATER. IF THAT WATER THEN EVAPORATES IN A BAG, I SHOULD STILL HAVE HALF AN OUNCE (10 G) OF WATER VAPOR (OR STEAM).

CHEMICAL CHANGES ARE A LITTLE MORE COMPLICATED. LET'S USE FOOD AS AN EXAMPLE. IF YOU TAKE A BEEF BURGER AND A CHICKEN SANDWICH AND SWITCH THE FILLINGS, YOU HAVE A BEEF SANDWICH AND A CHICKEN BURGER.

IF THE COMBINED WEIGHT OF THE BEEF BURGER AND CHICKEN SANDWICH IS 15 OZ (400 G), THEN THE COMBINED WEIGHT OF THE BEEF SANDWICH AND CHICKEN BURGER SHOULD STILL BE 15 OZ (400 G) BECAUSE NO NEW INGREDIENT WAS ADDED AND NO EXISTING INGREDIENT WAS LOST. SIMILARLY, IN CHEMISTRY, THE ELEMENTS (MATTER MADE OF JUST ONE TYPE OF ATOM) REARRANGE INTO NEW COMBINATIONS.

SINCE NOTHING WAS ADDED OR TAKEN AWAY, THIS SHOWS THAT MASS CANNOT BE CREATED OR DESTROYED, IT CAN ONLY CHANGE FROM ONE FORM TO ANOTHER. THIS IS CALLED THE LAW OF CONSERVATION OF MASS.

TING!

NOW, LET'S SEE WHAT HAPPENS WHEN WE APPLY THIS TO SUPERPOWERS.

BEANSTALK BOY:
LOOK AT HIM GROW!

If your best friend was being threatened by some bullies, wouldn't it be great to stand up to them at double your height?

BUT WAIT, AS WE JUST LEARNED ON PAGE 5, ALTHOUGH YOU ARE CHANGING SHAPE, YOU ARE NOT INCREASING IN MASS AND WOULD STILL WEIGH THE SAME. SO IF YOU ARE 70 LB (30 KG) AT YOUR NORMAL WEIGHT, WHEN YOU ARE TWICE AS TALL, YOU WOULD STILL ONLY WEIGH 70 LB (30 KG)? THAT CAN'T BE GOOD.

THIS IS JUST LIKE PUTTING A BALL OF PIZZA DOUGH IN A SEALED BAG AND ALLOWING IT TO RISE AND GET BIGGER. ITS MASS DOESN'T CHANGE BECAUSE THE DOUGH IS JUST GAINING AIR POCKETS.

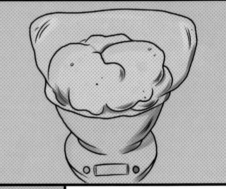

DENSER

SUGAR

IRON

THE PROBLEM IS, WHEN YOU INCREASE VOLUME (SIZE) WITHOUT INCREASING MASS, THE OVERALL DENSITY (THE MEASURE OF COMPACTNESS OF MATTER) DRAMATICALLY DECREASES. FOR EXAMPLE, IN THESE TWO CUBES OF THE SAME SIZE, THE IRON ATOMS ARE HEAVIER AND MORE COMPACTED THAN THE SUGAR ATOMS, SO MORE IRON ATOMS CAN FIT IN THE SAME SIZE CUBE.

BEANSTALK BOY'S SUPERPOWERS
- to grow to twice his size or more
- to reach high places
- to scare off bullies

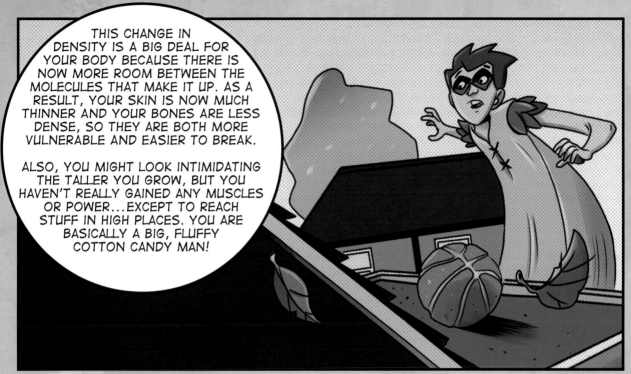

THIS CHANGE IN DENSITY IS A BIG DEAL FOR YOUR BODY BECAUSE THERE IS NOW MORE ROOM BETWEEN THE MOLECULES THAT MAKE IT UP. AS A RESULT, YOUR SKIN IS NOW MUCH THINNER AND YOUR BONES ARE LESS DENSE, SO THEY ARE BOTH MORE VULNERABLE AND EASIER TO BREAK.

ALSO, YOU MIGHT LOOK INTIMIDATING THE TALLER YOU GROW, BUT YOU HAVEN'T REALLY GAINED ANY MUSCLES OR POWER...EXCEPT TO REACH STUFF IN HIGH PLACES. YOU ARE BASICALLY A BIG, FLUFFY COTTON CANDY MAN!

CRUNCH!

LET'S SAY YOU CAN MAINTAIN A HUMAN'S AVERAGE DENSITY WHILE YOU ARE TWICE AS TALL. SO, WHEN YOU AREN'T IN SUPERHERO MODE, YOUR DENSITY WOULD BE DOUBLE, AND YOU'D WEIGH TWICE AS MUCH, AND HOPE NOBODY WOULD NOTICE.

WHOA!

DOUBLE THE HEIGHT, DOUBLE THE MASS, RIGHT? WELL, YES, BUT IF YOU DON'T WANT TO END UP LOOKING LIKE A STICKMAN, YOU'VE GOT TO APPLY THAT TO ALL THREE DIMENSIONS SO YOU ALSO BECOME WIDER AND THICKER.

THIS IS CALLED GALILEO'S SQUARE-CUBE LAW. SO WHEN YOU EXPAND PROPORTIONALLY TO TWICE YOUR HEIGHT, YOUR MASS WOULD ACTUALLY INCREASE 2 X 2 X 2 = 8 TIMES.

FOR EXAMPLE, IF YOU WANTED TO MAKE A CUBE TWICE THE HEIGHT OF A REGULAR CUBE, YOU WOULD NEED TO BUILD IT WITH FOUR CUBES FOR THE BASE AND ADD FOUR CUBES ON TOP TO REACH THE SAME HEIGHT.

ARRGH!

CAN YOU IMAGINE THE WEIGHT OF EIGHT OF YOU TRAPPED IN THE BODY OF ONE YOU? IF YOU EVER ACCIDENTALLY STEPPED ON SOMEBODY'S TOE, IT WOULD SEND THEM TO THE HOSPITAL!

EVER SEEN HIGH HEELS SINK INTO THE GROUND? THAT'S WHAT'S GOING TO HAPPEN TO YOU, BUT IT'LL HAPPEN TO YOUR WHOLE FOOT BECAUSE THE GROUND CAN'T TAKE THE PRESSURE OF YOUR BODY.

AND GOOD LUCK GETTING IN AN ELEVATOR WITH OTHER PEOPLE WITHOUT SETTING OFF THE ALARM!

MAXIMUM LOAD 10 PEOPLE

OH NO. MY CLOTHES!

RIIIIIIIP!

RIIIIIIIP!

RIIIIIIIP!

RIIIIIIIP!

THESE ARE JUST SOME OF THE PROBLEMS YOU WOULD FACE IN DAY-TO-DAY LIFE. WHEN YOU BECOME TWICE AS TALL AND YOUR BODY BECOMES EIGHT TIMES THE MASS, THERE WOULD BE A LOT OF OTHER PROBLEMS. FIRST OF ALL, HOW DO YOU KEEP YOUR CLOTHES FROM RIPPING?

PEOPLE WHO HAVE GONE THROUGH 1 FT (30 CM) GROWTH SPURTS WITHIN A THREE-MONTH PERIOD HAVE REPORTED EXPERIENCING EXCRUCIATING PAIN AND PERMANENT STRETCH MARKS ON THEIR BODIES. HOW DO YOU THINK YOUR BODY WOULD FEEL WHEN IT SUDDENLY EXPANDS WITHIN SECONDS? FOR STARTERS, YOUR BODY WOULD BE BLACK AND BLUE FROM THE VEINS BREAKING UNDER YOUR SKIN, FORMING BRUISES EVERYWHERE!

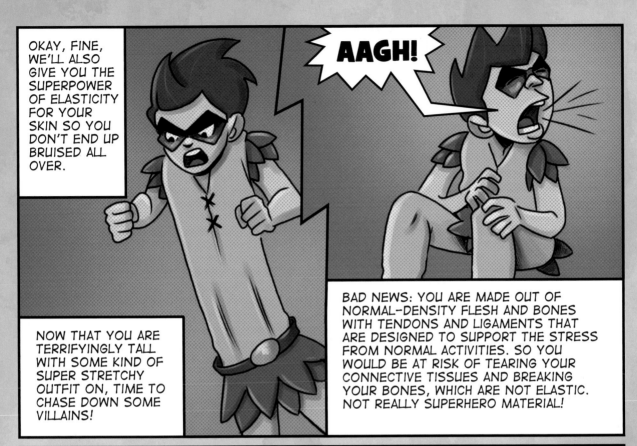

OKAY, FINE, WE'LL ALSO GIVE YOU THE SUPERPOWER OF ELASTICITY FOR YOUR SKIN SO YOU DON'T END UP BRUISED ALL OVER.

AAGH!

NOW THAT YOU ARE TERRIFYINGLY TALL WITH SOME KIND OF SUPER STRETCHY OUTFIT ON, TIME TO CHASE DOWN SOME VILLAINS!

BAD NEWS: YOU ARE MADE OUT OF NORMAL-DENSITY FLESH AND BONES WITH TENDONS AND LIGAMENTS THAT ARE DESIGNED TO SUPPORT THE STRESS FROM NORMAL ACTIVITIES. SO YOU WOULD BE AT RISK OF TEARING YOUR CONNECTIVE TISSUES AND BREAKING YOUR BONES, WHICH ARE NOT ELASTIC. NOT REALLY SUPERHERO MATERIAL!

WE WILL PROBABLY NEVER BE ABLE TO EXPAND AND GROW TO THE HEIGHT OF A BUILDING LIKE BEANSTALK BOY. BUT SCIENTIFIC STUDIES SHOW THAT HUMAN BEINGS HAVE BEEN STEADILY GROWING TALLER OVER THE PAST TWO HUNDRED YEARS ALL OVER THE WORLD.

OUCH!

SCIENTISTS THINK THIS IS DUE TO HUMAN BEINGS EATING BETTER AND BEING HEALTHIER DURING THIS PERIOD. SO WHO KNOWS? A FEW CENTURIES FROM NOW, THE AVERAGE HEIGHT MAY SOAR ANOTHER FOOT (30 CM)! AS WE'VE DISCOVERED IN THIS CHAPTER, TALLER IS NOT ALWAYS BETTER!

MICRO GIRL: SMALL BUT MIGHTY!

What if you could shrink down to the size of an insect? You'd be able to crawl into tight spaces and find people trapped after an earthquake!

ON MY WAY!

YOU COULD LISTEN IN ON SOME BAD GUYS' PLANS UNNOTICED AND STOP THEM BEFORE THEY CAN COMMIT A CRIME!

BUT THE PROBLEM IS: THE LAW OF CONSERVATION OF MASS WOULD STILL APPLY... THAT MEANS YOU WOULD REMAIN THE SAME WEIGHT BEFORE AND AFTER YOUR TRANSFORMATION. SO, ARE YOU ALWAYS 70 LB (30 KG) OR ARE YOU ALWAYS THE WEIGHT OF AN ANT (ONLY 1 TO 5 MG)?

MICRO GIRL'S SUPERPOWERS

- to shrink to the size of an insect
- to squeeze into tight spaces
- to go unnoticed

HELP ME, I FEEL A BREEZE COMING!

THAT MEANS YOU MUST ALWAYS WEIGH THE SAME AS A HUMAN GIRL. THE NEXT ISSUE YOU WOULD HAVE TO DEAL WITH WHILE WEIGHING 70 LB (30 KG) IN YOUR ANT-LIKE STATE IS YOUR BASIC ABILITY TO WALK ON SURFACES WITHOUT MAKING A DENT.

BEING A NORMAL-SIZED CHILD, YET WEIGHING ONLY AS MUCH AS AN ANT WOULD NOT BE PRACTICAL. AND WHEN YOU SHRINK, YOU'D BE TRAPPED UNDER THE HEAVY FABRIC OF YOUR EVERYDAY CLOTHES! AND YOU'D HAVE TO BE EXTRA CAREFUL ON A WINDY DAY! NOT GREAT FOR A SUPERHERO!

THE HEAVIER YOU ARE, THE MORE FORCE YOU APPLY TO THE GROUND YOU STAND ON. ONCE YOU SHRINK, YOUR FEET WOULD ALSO SHRINK TO, SAY, THE SIZE OF THE TIP OF A PIN. THIS MEANS THAT YOU ARE ONLY SUPPORTED BY AN AREA THE SIZE OF THE TIP OF A PIN. PRESSURE (A WAY OF MEASURING HOW MUCH FORCE IS ACTING OVER AN AREA) IS CALCULATED BY FORCE DIVIDED BY AREA: THE SMALLER THE AREA, THE GREATER THE PRESSURE BEING APPLIED TO WHAT YOU ARE STANDING ON AND THE STRONGER THE FORCE, THE STRONGER THE PRESSURE.

WHAT DO YOU THINK IS GOING TO HAPPEN WHEN YOU START WALKING ON THOSE TINY FEET OF YOURS WITH ALL 70 LB (30 KG) OF YOUR WEIGHT?

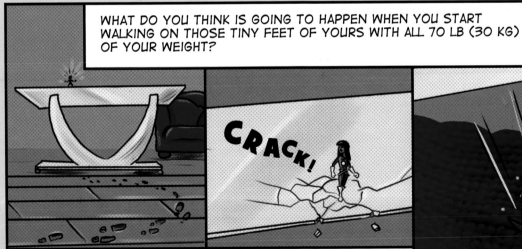

CRACK!

IF YOU WERE TO WALK ON WOODEN FLOORS, YOU WOULD LEAVE A TRAIL OF TINY FOOT DENTS. IF YOU WALKED ON A WOODEN TABLE, THE SAME THING WOULD HAPPEN.

ANY PIECE OF FURNITURE THAT IS NOT STURDY ENOUGH TO SUPPORT A HUMAN, LIKE A GLASS TABLE, WOULDN'T BE ABLE TO WITHSTAND THE PRESSURE EXERTED BY YOU.

AND IF YOU WALK ON A SOFA? WELL, YOUR WHOLE LEG WOULD DISAPPEAR AFTER YOUR FIRST STEP BECAUSE OF THE SOFTNESS OF THE SOFA CUSHION.

NOW LET'S LOOK AT SPEED. THE FASTEST RECORDED RUNNING HUMAN SPEED IS ABOUT 40 FT (10 M) PER SECOND. BUT EVEN IF YOU COULD RUN THAT FAST, SO WHAT?

PROPORTIONALLY, IF YOU ARE AS TALL AS A BIG ANT, THAT WOULD PUT YOUR SPEED AT AROUND 1 IN (2.5 CM) PER SECOND. TRUE, THAT'S TWICE THE SPEED OF THE AVERAGE SNAIL, BUT STILL NOT VERY FAST AT ALL.

IF YOU WANT TO RUN UP A BAD GUY'S ARM TO PUNCH HIM IN THE CHIN, YOU'LL FIND THAT YOU CAN'T. HE WOULDN'T BE ABLE TO LIFT HIS ARM WITH YOUR 70-LB (30-KG) WEIGHT ON IT, SO YOU'D BE CLIMBING UP HIS ARM LIKE IT WERE A MOUNTAIN.

LET'S IGNORE THE FACT THAT YOU ARE SO HEAVY THAT YOU WOULD PROBABLY SINK STRAIGHT THROUGH HIS ARM IF YOU STOOD ON IT, LEAVING FOOT DENTS IN HIS SKIN.

IN ORDER TO REACH HIS SHOULDERS FROM HIS FINGERTIPS, YOU WOULD HAVE TO RUN WHAT FEELS LIKE THE LENGTH OF TWO FOOTBALL FIELDS.

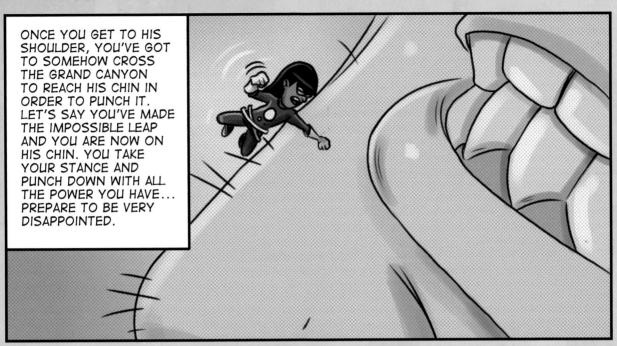

ONCE YOU GET TO HIS SHOULDER, YOU'VE GOT TO SOMEHOW CROSS THE GRAND CANYON TO REACH HIS CHIN IN ORDER TO PUNCH IT. LET'S SAY YOU'VE MADE THE IMPOSSIBLE LEAP AND YOU ARE NOW ON HIS CHIN. YOU TAKE YOUR STANCE AND PUNCH DOWN WITH ALL THE POWER YOU HAVE... PREPARE TO BE VERY DISAPPOINTED.

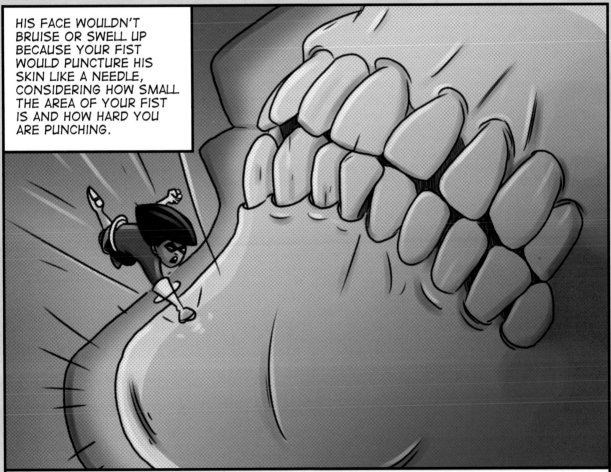

HIS FACE WOULDN'T BRUISE OR SWELL UP BECAUSE YOUR FIST WOULD PUNCTURE HIS SKIN LIKE A NEEDLE, CONSIDERING HOW SMALL THE AREA OF YOUR FIST IS AND HOW HARD YOU ARE PUNCHING.

REMEMBER, YOU ARE ONLY 0.2 IN (5 MM) TALL, SO YOUR ARM IS PROBABLY ONLY LESS THAN 0.1 IN (2 MM) LONG. THE THINNEST LAYER OF SKIN ON HIS BODY IS THICKER THAN YOUR ARM LENGTH.

EVEN THOUGH THE TECHNOLOGY IS NOT THERE TO SHRINK HUMAN BEINGS YET, WE HAVE BEEN REALLY SUCCESSFUL IN SHRINKING OUR DEVICES!

JUST THINK, WE HAVE MORE INFORMATION AND TECHNOLOGY AVAILABLE TO US ON ONE SMARTPHONE THAN OUR GRANDPARENTS HAD DURING THEIR ENTIRE CHILDHOODS.

EVEN GREATER ADVANCEMENTS ARE BEING MADE IN THE MEDICAL FIELD. INSTEAD OF OPENING PATIENTS UP IN LIFE-THREATENING SURGERIES, WHICH REQUIRE LONG RECOVERY TIMES, DOCTORS CAN NOW OPERATE BY MAKING VERY SMALL INCISIONS (CUTS). THEY INSERT EQUIPMENT, SUCH AS FIBER-OPTIC CAMERAS, INTO THE PATIENT'S BODY TO SEE WHAT'S WRONG AND WHERE TO OPERATE.

BELIEVE IT OR NOT, WE ARE NOW CAPABLE OF MAKING CAMERAS NO BIGGER THAN A GRAIN OF SALT! HMM, I WONDER WHAT ELSE WE CAN SHRINK...

CHAMELEA, THE SHAPE-SHIFTER:
WHO IS SHE?

Wouldn't it be great if you could change your shape? You'd be able to disguise yourself and walk past bad guys undetected!

OR CHANGE THE SHAPE OF OBJECTS TO SUIT YOUR NEEDS! LIKE TURNING YOUR SHOELACES INTO ROPES...

CHAMELEA'S SUPERPOWERS

- to change her appearance at will
- to change the shape of objects
- to make objects appear out of thin air

...OR EVEN CREATE SOMETHING OUT OF THIN AIR?

WOULDN'T IT BE GREAT TO HAVE WHATEVER OBJECT YOU WANT MATERIALIZE IN THE PALM OF YOUR HAND? YOU WOULD NEVER HAVE TO WORK FOR POCKET MONEY AGAIN!

POP!

POP!

BUT THERE'S SOMETHING IMPORTANT WE'VE MENTIONED BEFORE, WHICH MAKES THINGS COMPLICATED: CONSERVATION OF MASS...IT'S ACTUALLY A VERY SIMPLE CONCEPT: ANYTHING THAT HAS MASS AND TAKES UP SPACE CANNOT MAGICALLY APPEAR OR DISAPPEAR.

HEY PRESTO!

EVEN WHEN WE BURN THINGS AND THEY SEEMINGLY DISAPPEAR, THERE'S AN EXPLANATION FOR IT. IT MAY LOOK LIKE BURNING DESTROYS MATTER, BUT THE SAME AMOUNT, OR MASS, OF MATTER STILL EXISTS AFTER A CAMPFIRE AS BEFORE.

WHEN WOOD BURNS, IT COMBINES WITH OXYGEN AND CHANGES NOT ONLY INTO ASHES, BUT ALSO INTO CARBON DIOXIDE (CO_2) AND WATER VAPOR (H_2O). AS THE GASES FLOAT OFF INTO THE AIR, THE ONLY THING LEFT BEHIND IS THE ASHES.

SO IF YOU HAD MEASURED THE MASS OF THE WOOD BEFORE IT BURNED AND THE MASS OF THE ASHES AFTER IT BURNED, AND YOU WERE ABLE TO MEASURE THE OXYGEN USED BY THE FIRE AND THE GASES PRODUCED BY THE FIRE, WHAT WOULD YOU FIND? THE TOTAL MASS OF MATTER AFTER THE FIRE WOULD BE THE SAME AS THE TOTAL MASS OF MATTER BEFORE THE FIRE. BURNING DOES NOT DESTROY MATTER. IT JUST CHANGES MATTER INTO DIFFERENT SUBSTANCES.

AS THE FAMOUS FRENCH 18TH-CENTURY SCIENTIST ANTOINE LAVOISIER DISCOVERED:

NOTHING IS LOST. NOTHING IS CREATED. EVERYTHING IS TRANSFORMED.

SO IF YOU HAD THE POWER OF MATERIALIZATION AND MADE SOMETHING LIKE A PEN APPEAR OUT OF THIN AIR, YOU WOULD STILL HAVE TO EXPLAIN WHERE IT CAME FROM. ARE YOU REACHING INTO ANOTHER DIMENSION FOR THE EXTRA MATTER?

THE ISSUE OF EXTRA MATTER ALSO COMES UP WHEN YOU DECIDE TO PUT YOUR SHAPE-SHIFTING ABILITY TO SUPERHERO USE. YES, YOU WOULD BE ABLE TO CHANGE YOUR APPEARANCE TO LOOK LIKE WHOEVER YOU'D LIKE TO BE, BUT...

MYSTERY BELLE

SAY YOU TRANSFORMED INTO ONE OF THE BAD GUYS, YOU WOULD ALSO NEED CLOTHES THAT FIT WHO YOU'VE TRANSFORMED INTO. EVEN IF YOU WERE A SUPERHERO WHO COULD MAKE YOUR SKIN LOOK LIKE THEIR CLOTHES, THAT STILL ISN'T GOING TO WORK. YOU WOULDN'T BE ABLE TO TAKE OFF ANY PIECE OF CLOTHING SINCE IT'S ALL A PART OF YOU.

UMM, NO. THAT'S OKAY.

MAY I TAKE YOUR COAT?

OKAY, LET'S SAY YOU ARE ABLE TO STEAL THE BAD GUY'S CLOTHES EVERY TIME YOU GO ON A MISSION...

REMEMBER, YOU MAY BE CHANGING SHAPE BUT YOUR WEIGHT STAYS THE SAME. ALL PEOPLE WOULD HAVE TO DO IS WEIGH YOU AND THEY'D FIND OUT THAT YOU ARE NOT WHO YOU'RE MEANT TO BE!

JUST BECAUSE THERE'S ONE SHAPE-SHIFTER, NOW WE ALL HAVE TO STEP ON THE SCALES BEFORE ANY IMPORTANT MEETING? THIS IS RIDICULOUS.

YOU MIGHT RUN INTO OTHER PROBLEMS IF YOU USE YOUR SHAPE-SHIFTING ABILITY TO TURN INTO AN ANIMAL FOR A NIGHT, AND TURN BACK INTO A HUMAN IN THE MORNING. IF YOU DECIDED TO TURN INTO A WILD ANIMAL, SUCH AS A WOLF, YOU WOULD NEED TO BE CAREFUL NOT TO FALL INTO TOO MANY WOLF-LIKE HABITS.

GGRRRRRR!

A LARGE WOLF CAN EAT 20 LB (10 KG) OF MEAT IN ONE SITTING. THAT'S LIKE EATING TEN WHOLE ROAST CHICKENS FOR DINNER.

SLURP!

CRUNCH!

A HUMAN STOMACH CAN HOLD LESS THAN HALF THAT AMOUNT. SO, IF YOU EAT TOO MUCH THE NIGHT BEFORE, IN THE MORNING, YOUR HUMAN STOMACH IS GOING TO BURST!

WE MAY NEVER BE ABLE TO SHAPE-SHIFT OBJECTS OR OURSELVES IN THE SAME WAY CHAMELEA CAN. BUT CONSIDER WHAT HUMAN BEINGS HAVE BEEN ABLE TO DESIGN, BUILD, AND ENGINEER FROM MATERIALS AS BASIC AS ROCK AND MUD: WE HAVE MADE BOWLS, HOUSES, SKYSCRAPERS...

THESE OBJECTS AND STRUCTURES HAVE BECOME MORE AND MORE COMPLICATED OVER THE YEARS. ISN'T THAT THE REAL SUPERPOWER OF SHAPE-SHIFTING?

DISAPPEARING DENNIS: ONE MINUTE IN PARIS... THE NEXT IN VENICE!

Wouldn't it be great to have the power of teleportation?

BIFF!

YOU BLINK AND SUDDENLY YOU ARE BEHIND YOUR ENEMIES OR AT YOUR FAVORITE VACATION SPOT.

BUT WHAT ARE THE CONSEQUENCES OF COMING APART LIKE A PUFF OF SMOKE AND REASSEMBLING YOURSELF SOMEWHERE ELSE?

 ## DISAPPEARING DENNIS'S SUPERPOWERS

- to vanish and instantly appear somewhere else
- to be able to pass through matter

A PERSON CAN SUFFER FROM MEMORY LOSS AS A RESULT OF A HEAD INJURY. SO IF YOUR MEMORY CANNOT SURVIVE THE BLUNT TRAUMA OF AN ACCIDENT, HOW COULD IT EVER SURVIVE TOTAL DISASSEMBLY?

THE PROBLEM IS: ONCE YOU ARE TAKEN APART, YOU WILL NEVER BE THE SAME PERSON AGAIN BECAUSE THE CONNECTIONS IN YOUR BRAIN CANNOT BE REESTABLISHED. THINK ABOUT IT.

EVERY TIME YOU TELEPORT BY REASSEMBLY, YOUR FEELINGS, OPINIONS, EMOTIONS, PERSONALITY— EVERYTHING UNIQUE THAT MAKES YOU WHO YOU ARE— WOULD BE GONE!

YOU WOULD HAVE THE SAME PROBLEM IF YOU HAD THE POWER OF INTANGIBILITY (BEING ABLE TO GO THROUGH MATTER), ALLOWING YOU TO WALK THROUGH WALLS.

UNLESS YOU HAVE THE POWER TO FOLD SPACE AND MOVE THROUGH A PORTAL...

...YOU ARE BASICALLY SCANNING AND E-MAILING YOURSELF FROM ONE SPACE TO ANOTHER.

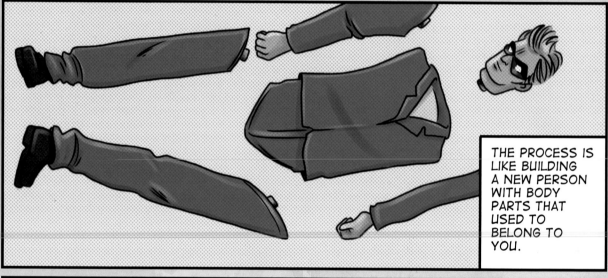

THE PROCESS IS LIKE BUILDING A NEW PERSON WITH BODY PARTS THAT USED TO BELONG TO YOU.

EVEN IF YOUR SUPERPOWERS ALLOWED YOU TO SOMEHOW RETAIN ANY SHRED OF WHAT MAKES YOU WHO YOU ARE, IF YOU WERE TO TELEPORT WITH A FRIEND, YOUR FRIEND WOULD LOSE THEIR MEMORIES FOR SURE.

WHO ARE YOU? WHERE AM I?

BESIDES, YOU ARE NEVER TRULY ALONE. THE NUMBER OF BACTERIA LIVING ON YOU ACTUALLY OUTNUMBER YOUR CELLS BY 10 TO 1.

SO FOR EVERY ONE OF YOUR HUMAN CELLS, THERE ARE 10 BACTERIA CELLS. THEY ARE RESPONSIBLE FOR YOUR HEALTH, INCLUDING YOUR DIGESTIVE SYSTEM. SO THEY ARE YOUR FRIENDS.

NOW, WHEN YOU TELEPORT, DO YOU BRING THEM ALONG? OR DO THEY STAY PUT? IF TELEPORTATION IS LIMITED TO TRANSPORTING YOU AND ONLY YOU, THESE ESSENTIAL BACTERIA WOULD BE LEFT BEHIND. MAYBE THAT'S WHAT THE PUFF OF SMOKE IS MADE OUT OF?

OOPS!

ALSO, YOUR CLOTHES ARE NOT REALLY PART OF YOU. THAT MEANS YOU WOULD BE TELEPORTING COMPLETELY NAKED! THAT COULD BE AWKWARD...

ANOTHER THING: WHAT IF YOU MISCALCULATED THE SPACE YOU WERE TELEPORTING TO AND ENDED UP PICKING A BAD SPOT? WOULD YOU BE SQUEEZED INTO THE SPACE FOREVER?

HELP!

UH OH!

AAGGH!

OR WORSE, WHAT IF YOUR BODY CELLS MERGED WITH WHATEVER WAS THERE TO CREATE A HALF-HUMAN HALF-ITEM HYBRID FOREVER? YIKES!

TELEPORTATION MAY REMAIN A THING OF FICTION FOR A LONG TIME, IF NOT FOREVER. HOWEVER, ADVANCES IN TRANSPORTATION, SUCH AS AIRPLANES AND HIGH-SPEED TRAINS, HAVE MADE TRAVELING A LOT MORE COMFORTABLE, RELIABLE, EFFICIENT, AND FASTER THAN IT WAS A FEW CENTURIES AGO.

FASTER STILL THAN ACTUALLY GOING TO FARAWAY PLACES, YOU CAN NOW VIDEO CALL ANYONE WITH A SMARTPHONE OR A COMPUTER ANYWHERE IN THE WORLD.

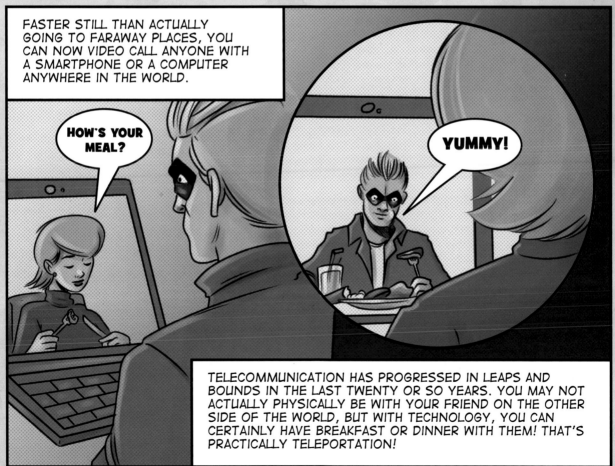

HOW'S YOUR MEAL?

YUMMY!

TELECOMMUNICATION HAS PROGRESSED IN LEAPS AND BOUNDS IN THE LAST TWENTY OR SO YEARS. YOU MAY NOT ACTUALLY PHYSICALLY BE WITH YOUR FRIEND ON THE OTHER SIDE OF THE WORLD, BUT WITH TECHNOLOGY, YOU CAN CERTAINLY HAVE BREAKFAST OR DINNER WITH THEM! THAT'S PRACTICALLY TELEPORTATION!

GLOSSARY

atoms THE BUILDING BLOCKS OF MATTER

bond A LINK BETWEEN ATOMS THAT HAVE JOINED TOGETHER

condensation WHEN A GAS TURNS INTO A LIQUID

conservation THE ACTION OF KEEPING SOMETHING RELATIVELY THE SAME

density HOW HEAVY SOMETHING IS FOR ITS SIZE, THE MEASURE OF COMPACTNESS OF MATTER

deposition WHEN A GAS TURNS INTO A SOLID

disassembly THE PROCESS OF COMING APART

elasticity THE ABILITY OF AN OBJECT OR MATERIAL TO RETURN TO ITS ORIGINAL FORM AFTER BEING STRETCHED OR SQUEEZED

element MATTER MADE OF JUST ONE TYPE OF ATOM

evaporation WHEN A LIQUID TURNS INTO A GAS

fiber optic A METHOD OF TRANSMITTING LIGHT THROUGH FINE, TRANSPARENT, FLEXIBLE STRANDS, USUALLY MADE OF GLASS OR PLASTIC

freezing WHEN A LIQUID TURNS INTO A SOLID

frequency (sound) NUMBER OF SOUND WAVES OR VIBRATIONS IN A SECOND

fusion WHEN A SOLID MELTS AND TURNS INTO A LIQUID

gas MATTER THAT HAS NO DEFINITE SIZE OR SHAPE BECAUSE THE MOLECULES THAT CONSTITUTE IT ARE MOVING FAST AND ARE WIDELY SPREAD OUT. ONE OF THE THREE MAIN STATES OF MATTER

hybrid SOMETHING THAT IS A MIXTURE OF TWO VERY DIFFERENT THINGS

incision SURGICAL CUT MADE IN THE SKIN OR FLESH

intangibility NOT HAVING A PHYSICAL PRESENCE, UNABLE TO BE TOUCHED

liquid MATTER THAT HAS A DEFINITE SIZE BUT NO DEFINITE SHAPE BECAUSE THE ATOMS THAT CONSTITUTE IT ARE LOOSELY LINKED. ONE OF THE THREE MAIN STATES OF MATTER

mass THE AMOUNT OF MATTER IN AN OBJECT

materialize APPEAR AND BECOME ACTUAL OBJECTS

matter ANYTHING THAT HAS MASS AND TAKES UP SPACE. IT IS THE STUFF THAT ALL OBJECTS AND MATERIALS AROUND US ARE MADE OF

molecules UNITS OF MATTER MADE OF ATOMS BONDED TOGETHER

pressure A WAY OF MEASURING HOW MUCH FORCE IS ACTING OVER AN AREA

rise IN THE CASE OF DOUGH, TO SWELL AND BECOME BIGGER BECAUSE YEAST ARE MULTIPLYING

shape-shift THE ABILITY TO CHANGE PHYSICAL FORM AT WILL

solid MATTER THAT HAS A DEFINITE SIZE AND SHAPE BECAUSE THE ATOMS THAT CONSTITUTE IT ARE TIGHTLY PACKED. ONE OF THE THREE MAIN STATES OF MATTER

sound wave THE FORM THAT SOUND TAKES WHEN IT PASSES THROUGH AIR OR WATER

states of matter THE FORMS MATTER CAN EXIST IN: SOLID, LIQUID, GAS, OR THE VERY RARE FORM—PLASMA

sublimation WHEN A SOLID TURNS INTO A GAS

telecommunication THE PROCESS OF COMMUNICATING OVER DISTANCES VIA TELEPHONE, THE INTERNET, OR E-MAIL

teleport MOVE ACROSS SPACE AND DISTANCE INSTANTLY

trauma SEVERE INJURY CAUSING EMOTIONAL SHOCK

volume THE AMOUNT OF SPACE SOMETHING TAKES UP

weight THE FORCE CAUSED BY GRAVITY AND MEASURED IN NEWTONS. THE WEIGHT OF AN OBJECT IS HOW HARD GRAVITY PULLS DOWN ON IT

FURTHER INFORMATION

WEBSITES

www.bbc.co.uk/bitesize/ks2/science/materials
GAMES AND REVISION ABOUT MATERIALS AND THE STATES OF MATTER

www.chem4kids.com/files/matter_intro.html
A WEBSITE THAT EXPLAINS MATTER IN MORE DEPTH

www.youtube.com/playlist?list=PLhz12vamHOnaY7nvpgtQ0SIbuJdC4HA5O
A FUN PLAYLIST OF CRASH COURSE KIDS VIDEOS ABOUT MATTER AND ITS PROPERTIES

https://ed.ted.com/series/?series=superhero-science
AUTHOR JOY LIN'S TED ED VIDEOS ABOUT SCIENCE AND SUPERHEROES

https://www.khanacademy.org/science/chemistry/states-of-matter-and-intermolecular-forces/states-of-matter/v/states-of-matter
A WEBSITE THAT PROVIDES AN INTRODUCTION TO THE STATES OR PHASES OF MATTER

BOOKS

Mind Webs: Materials BY ANNA CLAYBOURNE (WAYLAND, 2014)

Science in a Flash: States of Matter
BY GEORGIA AMSON-BRADSHAW (FRANKLIN WATTS, 2017)

Science Makers: Making with States of Matter
BY ANNA CLAYBOURNE (WAYLAND, 2018)

Moving Up with Science: Matter BY PETER RILEY (FRANKLIN WATTS, 2016)

INDEX